new big green annual

by john beasley

additional pictures

chris cook   P.29 Howsyourluck, P.49 Global Legend (2), P.77 Kinnefad King, P.106 Upton Adventure, P.111 High Bridge, P.112 Snow, The Crazy Bishop, P.132 Smile Pleeze, P.133 Sun Surfer, P.153 Nothing Ventured.

john grossick   P.13 Dennett Lough, Da Silva, P15. More Joy, P25. Maximize (2), Easterby, P.35 Pebble Beach,Wilson,Walton, P.56 Shay Gap, P57. Carlinare, P.62 Col. Hogg, P63 Hutton Rudby, P.64 Rainbow Times, Judges, P.65 Pharmistice, Alexander, P.67 Cool Yule, Kyle, P.73 Parade Racer, P.125 Balisteros, P.128 Little Brockwell, P.129 Riverside Run, Pharmistice, P139. Storey, P.158 Balisteros.

david strange   P.8 Quick Response, P.26 Bookies, P.48 Summitt, Gluvum, P.76 Mr Kevernair, P.106 Highway Lad, P.123 Nuns Cone, P.138 Hutsby, P.117 Peafield.

associate editor: david briers

design by bobco

printed by Cambrian Printers
Llanbadarn Road Aberystwyth SY23 3TN

first published in great britain by paleface publications
30 thistlebarrow road bournemouth dorset BH7 7AL 01202 309489

The moral right of the author has been asserted.

ISBN 0-9539608-0-3

new big green annual

season 2000

contents

3

Above: Balisteros and Pauline Robson with owner Billie Thomson after recording his first win of the season at Tweseldown in Hampshire.

january

Above: The low January sun streams across the parade ring at Tweseldown as the Thames Valley Club Veteran and Novice riders prepare to mount on the first day of the season.

BRILLIANT Balisteros! That was the story not only in the Northern area but throughout the rest of the country as Billie Thomson's pride and joy enjoyed a spectacular season that began for the gelding on the opening day and lasted until June, something that speaks volumes for the horse's durability and enthusiasm.

The 11-year-old ran 17 times, winning 10 point-to-points and three hunter chases as well as being placed in his other four outings (second in two hunter chases and third in two points).

Right: Robert Biddlecombe becomes a winning rider at his first attempt as he guides Rectory Garden over the last in the Veterans' and Novice Riders' race at Tweseldown.
Below: Robert with proud father and racing legend Terry Biddlecombe.

Left: Rob Mine wears the rug of sponsors William Hill Organisation Ltd in the winner's enclosure after his Men's Open victory in the hands of Simon Sporborg (inset) at Tweseldown.

Above: First fence action at Tweseldown in the Open Maiden race sponsored by the Royal Bank of Scotland where Straight Baron (Chris Gordon) left, Billy Blakeney (Rowan Cope), and Sixth Sense (Paul McAllister) right, dispute the lead.

That dazzling record included wins on consecutive days on two occasions. And his successes were not all clocked up in his own back yard because on the first day of the campaign owner/trainer Billie and rider Pauline Robson embarked on a marathon trip of more than 700 miles to raid the Thames Valley Club fixture at Tweseldown in north Hampshire.

7

Above: Smart Orange, left, Gaelic Royale and Coddington Girl, right, dispute the lead during the Restricted race at the Point-to-Point Owners' & Riders' Club meeting at Barbury Castle near Marlborough, Wiltshire.

Below: Quick Response gives Melanie Nordledge a diving fall after being hampered at the first fence in the Maiden race division two at the PPORA Club meeting.

Four out you would not have given a jot for their chances in the Ladies' race but Pauline, told to bide her time until the last moment, knew better and produced Balisteros with a storming late run to snatch the verdict in the final 50 yards, a performance that thrilled the 5,000-plus crowd on a sun-drenched January day.

Balisteros never ventured as far south again - though there would

Above: The irrepressible Alex Charles-Jones guards the make-up box in a crowded changing room at Barbury Castle.

Right: Barbury Castle winner Becky Curtis.

have been a hefty cash bonus from bookmakers William Hill had he done so and triumphed again at the Hampshire circuit - but he did make his mark with victories at National Hunt tracks Kelso, Sedgefield and Uttoxeter as well as a close second to the impressive Lord Harry in the John Corbett Cup at Stratford on June 2.

Above: Touchdown on Salisbury Plain as runners stream over the thirst last fence during a Ladies' Open race at Larkhill, Wiltshire.

Left: Owner Richard Crabb, right, and COH Owen Cornock with the Mounted Infantry Cup after Knight of Passion won the Beer Sellers Ladies' Open race at Larkhill.

On home ground Balisteros featured in arguably the area's finest race when, ridden by Jill Wormall, he quickened over the last two fences to outgun Pharmistice and Pauline Robson on Riparius in the Ladies' Open at the Lauderdale.

That heroic effort looked even better since just the previous day

Above: Professional lady jockey Sophia Mitchell gives her brothers Nick, left, and Tim, right, the benefit of her wisdom after their Titanic battle for the Maiden race division two spoils at Larkhill.

Right: Larkhill winner Leslie Jefford.

Balisteros, this time with Pauline in the saddle, had been forced to pull out all the stops to sweep past Val Jackson on Storm Alive on the run-in to grab the Ladies' prize at Aspatria.

Balisteros had not cut any ice under Rules - or when an inmate of the Richard Barber stable for that matter - and his memorable season not only showed how much a horse can benefit from individual handling in a smaller yard but also how even at a double-figure age improvement can still be achieved.

Above: Bally Clover, ridden by Lawney Hill, leads Just Like Madge (Jimmy Tarry) and Free to Conker (Mark Hawkins, 7) during the Lloyds' Chemist Club Members' race at Mollington.

Below: Whistling Rufus (Mark Rimell), left, Romany Chat (Andy Martin) and Tellaporky (Emma Owen), right, line abreast at the second last during the NH Trainers' Club Members' Confined Maiden race at Mollington.

Above: NH trainer Robin Dickin with winning owners Claud Bosley, right, and Mr and Mrs Richard Vaughan after Severn Magic won at Mollington.

*Above: Dennett Lough puts in a fine leap under Clive
Storey as they lead Lottery Ticket (Simon Robinson) to
win the Men's Open at Alnwick in Northumberland.*

*Right: David Da Silva and Jane
Hollands with Manhattan Rainbow
who gave him a win on his first ride
in the Maiden at Alnwick.*

Pauline Robson's association with Balisteros was perfect - they landed five wins out of five appearances together - and this helped her take the area ladies' title for the ninth time. Clive Storey scooped the men's crown for the third year running, both champions riding 21 winners apiece though some of those were out of the area.

Above: Running repairs at Larkhill where gale force winds gusting across Salisbury Plain threatened to blow the Stewards' room roof off.

Above: Pals Willy Pearce and Taffy Austin, right, enjoy a tipple on a cold day at Larkhill.

Right: Reigning champion Julian Pritchard all smiles after Fresh Prince won The Honourable Artillery Company Mixed open race division two at Larkhill.

Storey's large string again had a highly successful campaign and this contributed almost entirely towards the College Valley and North Northumberland Hunt easily winning the John Swan and Son Inter-Hunt award for the first time.

There were several contenders for the novice riders' championship which eventually went to Mathew

Above: More Joy and Sean Bowden lead the Maiden field from Dram Hurler (Ranold Morgan), Superior Weapon and Smiddy Lad at Alnwick.

Above: Larkhill winner Paul Cowley.

Below: Trainer Alex Hales.

Above: Phillip York still smiling after a narrow escape during a Maiden race at Larkhill.

Below: Barry Kendellan after his Larkhill win on Coach in the Members' race.

Clayton with five victories, all of them from Ian and Anne Hamilton's Claywalls stable. Mathew has now joined Micky Hammond's racing yard under Rules and will be out to make a name for himself as an amateur.

Among eye-catching young horses to make their debuts during the season were Divet Hill, Sunnycliff, Dere Street and the five-year-old mare Wills Perk, all of them winners.

15

Above: Novice riders Mair Lowndes, left, and Patrick Dartnall, right, in action at Barbury Castle during the GriffinNuu-Med Point-to-Point Owners & Riders' Club Members' race.

Below: Doctor Cave swings into action after Robert Cooper took a heavy fall from Manamour during the Sean Graham Mixed Open race at Barbury Castle.

Above: First race on the card at Barbury Castle, the Weatherbys' Point-to-Point Owners' & Riders' Club Maiden race where Dozmary Poole (Richard Burton) leads True Hustler (Fred Hutsby) and eventual winner We Move Earth, right, with Polly Gundry in the saddle.

Teenager Robert Walford marked his arrival in the Wessex area with a double and a 100 fine during the Army fixture at Larkhill.

Robert Alner's stable amateur guided Aberfoyle Park and River Swilley to slender victories in divisions of the Maiden and Restricted respectively, both by three-quarters of a length, for Robert's daughter Louise.

17

Above: Impressive pointer Real Value and Ben Hitchcott, right, jump with eventual winner Secret Bay (Ben Pollock) during the Land Rover Men's Open at Cottenham in Cambridgeshire.

Left: Tim Lane becomes the centre of attention after his mount Give it a Whirl fell during the Intermediate race at Cottenham.

Right: Mark Munrowd.

But when Walford was pipped by Highway Lad by exactly the same distance on Chism in the Men's Open, he incurred the wrath of the stewards who stung him in the pocket for failing to ride out the nine-year-old.

Another teenager Charlotte Tizzard stole the limelight at Barbury Castle in January when

Above: Stalls to the right, Circle to the left. The segregated grandstand at Cottenham in January.

Above:
Lucy Watson.

Below:
Rachel Clark.

Above: Charlie Lane. Point-to-Point controller, at Tweseldown on day one of the 2000 season.

she started what proved to be a wonderful partnership this year with Millyhenry. The gelding notched eight wins this season, seven of them in the very capable hands of Charlotte who took the second division of the Novice Riders' race by 10 lengths at the Point-to-point Owners' and Riders' Club fixture.

19

Right: Leading lady rider Shirley Vickery strays into the Gentlemen's changing room at Larkhill and in no time two pairs of trousers fall down.

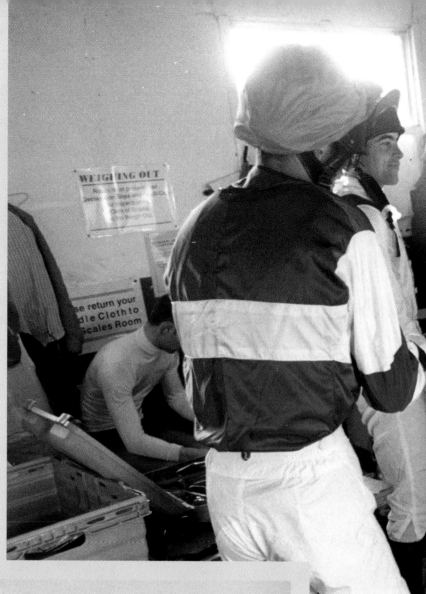

Below: Catachan (Mark Rimmel) left, and Goforitgirl (Les Jefford) lead the Maiden race division one field at Larkhill with eventual winner Aberfoyle Park and Robert Walford in close company. Shirley Vickery on No Loss, left, finished second.

Tabitha Cave was the other successful partner on Millyhenry stepping in for a chance ride at Cothelstone during a day of record-breaking times at the Quantock Staghounds meeting after Charlotte had taken a heavy fall in the Ladies' Open on the firm ground.

In contrast to young talents

Walford and Tizzard when the Royal Artillery held their fixture at Larkhill was John Mead.
 The 57-year-old owner/rider savoured success in the Maiden on Lost Your Marbles, the only time the seven-year-old mare showed any real sparkle during a campaign which saw her fail to finish seven times out of ten.

Above: Punters enjoy the Sunday sunshine at Charing in Kent where the South East Hunts Club race.

Left: Honorary secretary Sue Addington-Smith (third left) and some of her volunteers at Charing.

Leslie Jefford carried off the men's national championship this year but his hopes took a bad knock literally at the Royal Artillery meeting when Country Captain suffered a fatal heart attack during the first division of the Maiden leaving his rider with a damaged collarbone.

Robert Biddlecombe - 17-year-old son of former champion National Hunt jockey Terry - looks a very stylish addition to the riders' ranks. His dad confessed

february

Above: The end of another busy day at Buckfastleigh in Devon and as the winter sun casts long shadows across the course the scales head back into storage.

to having a tear in his eye when Robert won the opening ride of his career at Tweseldown in January on Rectory Garden, a gelding owned by Terry.

The combination quickly chalked up a treble (at Barbury Castle and a return trip to Tweseldown in Hampshire) before finally meeting their match in a frantic finish to the Coronation Cup, highlight of the United Services' fixture at Larkhill on Salisbury Plain in Wiltshire.

Above: Bolshie Baron and Jamie Jukes (5), A Few Dollars More (Richard Woollacott) and eventual winner Bally Wirral under Godfrey Maundrell all full of running early in the Mountpleasant Inn Intermediate race at Chipley Park in Somerset.

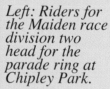

Left: Riders for the Maiden race division two head for the parade ring at Chipley Park.

Right: Roy Emmett at Chipley Park.

Victory went to Ruperts Choice and Simon Sporborg by a rapidly dwindling margin after young Robert had applied the waiting tactics perhaps a little too long. The official verdict at the line was a neck.

The grandly named Larkhill

Top: Maximize wins the Maiden at Friars Haugh giving Clive Storey a four-timer and, above, a delighted trainer Ian Stark in the winner's enclosure.

Right: David Easterby steers Jackson's Hole over the last to win the Restricted Open race at Sinnington.

National - a four-mile mixed open staged during the Staff College & RMA Sandhurst Draghounds date - saw a thrilling triumph for 19-year-old Caroline Tuffin aboard her only horse Blue Laws. The winner is bred in the pink, being by Bluebird out of a Roberto mare, and relished every yard of the marathon journey.

Above;Bookies at Wadebrige in Cornwall utilize the Royal Corn-wall showground buildings.

Left; Saxon Fair and Gary Hanmer lead Forest Fountain (Julian Pritchard) during the Armstrong& Co. Mens Open race at Whitwick Manor.

As the field approached the home straight, any one of five could have prevailed and Blue Laws, who had been making stealthy progress, shot through on the outside with his young rider holding off The Hobbit by a length in a driving finish.

Tim Mitchell, leading the championship race at the time, suffered a broken collarbone in a tumble from Snowshill Harvest.

Above: Happen To Make It and Julian Pritchard lead, left to right, Romany Chat (Andy Martin), Strong Accent (Robert Sealey), Musical Hit (Charlie Wadland) and Uncle Reginald (Bruce McKim) on the home turn, first circuit, during the Dowdeswell Confined Maiden race division two at Dunthrop.

Right: Richard Hunnisett with the impressive Steggles Palmer trophy after winning the Men's Open at Dunthrop on his brilliant jumper Copper Thistle, left.

Left: Point-to-point legend Joe Turner relaxes for a few minutes during a busy meeting at Charing in Kent.

Below: Leading South East rider Andrew Hickman at Charing.

The emphatic victory of Harry Wellstead's five-year-old caused both owner and winning rider Walford to be interviewed by the stewards in view of the gelding's performance at the United Services meeting where he was pulled up.

The explanation that Walford had called a halt to that first outing after the horse had suffered cuts to his legs and was unable to gallop properly was accepted.

Polly Gundry's triumph in the women's national title race

Right: Howsy-ourLuck and Tim Vaughan, right, lead Saxon Queen (Evan Williams) to win the Confined maiden race at Erw Lon in Carm-arthenshire.

Above: Teeton Builds and Andrew Sansome, centre, jump with eventual winner Real Value (Andrew Hickman), left, with Bang on Target and Nadjati hard on their heels during the Hobbs Parker Men's Open race at Charing.

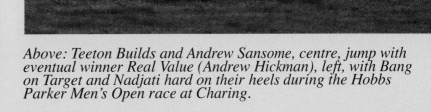

Above: The men's changing room at Charing.

owed much to her link with the Richard Barber stable and never better was this demonstrated than on the trainer's local course Littlewindsor at the Seavington meeting where she rode a treble.

She scored on the newcomer Rimpton Boy (five to seven-year-old Maiden, two and a half miles), Dannicus (Ladies' Open) and My Clean Sweep (Restricted). But her feat was matched by Nick Mitchell who also rattled up a three-timer on the course.

Above: Another big field at Dunthrop where Mr Custard, ridden by Lucinda Sweeting (red and grey colours), just lead Over The Master (David Barlow), left, King Of Clare (Andy Martin), True Chimes (James Owen) and Le Meille (Edward Walker), right, during the Countryside Assurance Group Confined race.

Mitchell's winners were Franklins Best (Members), Basil (three-mile Maiden) and Noddadante (Open) which is owned by his father Richard Mitchell.

Leslie Jefford reached the milestone of 100 winners during Blackmore & Sparkford Vale's date at Charlton Horethorne on bargain-buy Elliewelliewoo who

made it three in a row to continue the unbeaten start to her career in the Intermediate. The seven-year-old was in with a good chance of notching a fourth victory in May when taking on the redoubtable Butler John at Lifton but she lost her bridle after a mistake when in contention and Jefford pulled her up.

Above: Ruins dominate the centre of the new course at Chipley Park.

Above: Pachakutec, ridden by Richard Woollacott leads Tiger Bell (Scarlett Major) during the Lionel Redwood Memorial Open race division two at Chipley Park.

Above: Winners, Philelwyn and Adrian Wintle (green cap), jump with Missed Call and All Things Nice at Whitwick Manor during the Technicrop Confined Maiden race.

Left: Andrew Dalton and Mickthe-cutaway after winning the Men's Open race and the Heygate Gold Cup at Whitwick Manor near Hereford.

Below: Stewards John de Lisle, left, and John Weston on duty at Whitwick Manor.

That was Butler John's 25th career win and Gerald Dartnall's star went on to round off his season with triumph number 26 less than a week later on home ground at Bratton Down.

Polly Gundry hotted up the title race with a treble at the Portman, two of them saddled by Richard Barber.

33

Above: Energetic spectators gain a panoramic view of racing from the hill at Buckfastleigh in Devon.

Above: Maiden race winner Brother Nero with Mark and Yvonne Watson, lass Justine Baker, rider Colin Heard and Rupert Huddy of Sponsors Ham & Huddy at Buckfastleigh.

Left: Leading lady rider Rilly Goschen at Buckfastleigh.

Watched by a massive Badbury Rings crowd she drove Abit More Business to foil Stoney River on the line in the Confined and then weighed in with Mizyan (Mixed Open) and Bright Approach (Intermediate).

The rain-soaked Taunton Vale day at Kingston St Mary was significant in that Polly's double on one-time invalid Kingsbridge

Above: Pebble Beach and Celia Savell take a plain fence during the Ladies' Open race at Alnwick.

Right: Alnwick winner Chris Wilson after Quarterstaff's victory in the Restricted race.

Above: Jimmy Walton receives the Hunt Challenge Bowl from Samantha Watson after winning the Men's Open at Alnwick.

(Members) and Mizyan (Ladies) put her two ahead of Pip Jones in the ladies' championship.

Schoolboy Hugo Froud scored the first win of his pointing life during the Weston and Banwell Harriers fixture at Cothelstone.

The 16-year-old pupil at King's School, Bruton, Somerset, took the Novice Riders' on former smart NH chaser Amtrak Express who was third in the 1996 Whitbread Gold Cup for Nicky Henderson.

Left: Caroline Head, collector of paddock numbers at Dunthrop.

Below: Course inspector and former leading National Hunt jockey Richard Linley with trainer Walter Dennis, right, at Buckfastleigh.

Right: Fence stewards Fred Gwilliam, left, and Sam Meredith on duty at fence six, Whitwick Manor.

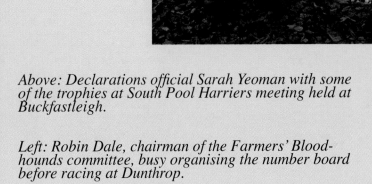

Above: Declarations official Sarah Yeoman with some of the trophies at South Pool Harriers meeting held at Buckfastleigh.

Left: Robin Dale, chairman of the Farmers' Bloodhounds committee, busy organising the number board before racing at Dunthrop.

Above: All eyes on the action as a massive crowd turns out for the marathon ten race card at Whitwick Manor which included the prestigious Heygate Gold Cup.

Above: Philip Hall enters the history books as the first rider to fall at Rodmell after Just Try Mr failed to complete the course in the Peter Edwards Hunt race.

Right: Stewards John Cory, left, Jim Thomas and Major John Anderson, right, oversee proceedings in the parade ring at Llanfrynach in Wales where a record 14 races took place.

In East Anglia it was a blooming good season - as far as Nibby Bloom was concerned. After several less than successful campaigns by his own high standards, he booted home 18 winners to scoop the title of champion jockey for the area.

His finest hour came at Fakenham's West Norfolk meeting.

Sense Of Adventure was never jumping fluently or travelling on the bridle in the Confined yet

march

Above: Rusty Buck (Steve Blackwell) leads the Restricted race division one field into the home straight on the first circuit at Llanfrynach near Brecon.

Nibby refused to accept defeat and pushing and cajoling almost from flagfall he kept the short-priced favourite in contention
 Vying for the lead when another ponderous jump seemed to have sealed his fate at the last, Nibby squeezed Sense Of Adventure through the narrowest of gaps along the stands rails without picking up his stick to collar Mister Audi on the line.

Above: No way back for Mouse Barlow as Another Junior gets it all wrong three from home in the NFU Restricted race at Badbury Rings in Dorset.

Above: Chiaroscuro and Steve Lloyd, far side, jump alongside Sebastopol (Grant Lewis) with eventual winner Red Neck, ridden by Tim Vaughan, in third place during the de Winton Memorial Confined race at Llanfrynach.

Left: Thomas Faulkener at Llanfrynach.

That was the first leg of a memorable 146-1 four-timer for Nibby who completed his quartet aboard Tod's Brother in a division of the Maiden bringing the 37-year-old's career total between the flags to 150 winners.

The personable Nibby is a fine ambassador for the sport - as is Zoe Turner, who became the area's leading lady rider.

Right: Brecon where decent handbrakes are required on the hillside parking area.

Below: The judge's young assistants wait for the action to begin.

Above: Number board lady Marcia Hullis struggles in the biting wind at High Easter in Essex during the Easton Harriers meeting.

Based at the family's yard near Bury St Edmunds Zoe has returned to the saddle after breaking her neck in a fall at Charing a few years ago.

But she finally gained the reward that her labours deserved with a first area triumph. Her success was founded upon her association with the enigmatic Spring Gale, who did not look the easiest of rides and had defeated the training talents of

Above: Fiona Jonason, last minute adjustments at High Easter.

Below: Anne-Marie Hays and Gi d'Angibau wait in the freezing wind at High Easter following a delayed start to the Harpers and Queens Ladies' Open race.

Venetia Williams under Rules. However, Spring Gale left his dubious past behind with a sparkling campaign that saw him chalk up six victories, often with great ease.

Another jockey to shine was Christian Ward-Thomas who rattled up a dozen wins and particularly excelled aboard the hair-raising front-runner Dry Highline.

Left: Summit and Jane Congdon part company at the ditch during the Mixed Open race division two at Buckfastleigh

Right: The flying grey Glevum and Tom Scuda-more, right, jump with Arctic Pearl (Robert Langley) to win the Mares' Club race at Siddington.

There was laughter aplenty from the chasing pack as Dry Highline set a scorching pace at Ampton in January hurling himself at his fences. But the smiles were wiped off those mocking faces when the Dry Dock gelding held off a determined late challenge from Tom De Savoie to win.

A few weeks later many thought Christian had again taken leave of his senses as Dry Highline began

Above: Global Legend and Adrian Wintle take a plain fence in fine style to win the Members race at Garnons near Hereford.

Right: The delighted connections of Global Legend line up with their charge after winning the Members at Garnons.

at break-neck speed over heavy ground at Marks Tey.

Yet his rivals obviously had not heeded the Ampton lesson and the front-runner trotted up by a comfortable 20 lengths.

The dashing tactics, however, did not always pay dividends as three times in as many months at Cottenham the partnership became victims of the island fence and ended up in a heap.

49

6TH RACE

3	A. COE	19	C. GORDON
4	MR. S. SPORBORG	20	M. GINGELL
5	D. COOK	24	N. BLOOM
6	W. WALES	26	A. SANSOME
9	T. LANE	29	N. KING
11	C. O'BRIEN	30	R. FOWLER
14	A. BRAITHWAITE	31	A. HARVEY
15	MRS. S. HODGE	32	R. ROSS
16	D. PAGE	33	G. LUSH
17	P. ELLISON		

Focus on Horseheath in Cambridgeshire: Easy access via the A604, above, the excellent number board, left, and, below, the gentlemen's conveniences...

Newcomers to the winner's enclosure included Catherine Tuke, Caroline Fryer and Andrew Ayers but the fresh face who really caught the eye was 16-year-old Matthew Abrey.

He made a winning debut on Dockmaster in the Men's Open at Higham during February and staged a repeat performance on the same horse the following month giving the impression that here is a

Above: Andrelot and Coral Grissell lead Black Book and Anna Burton at the ditch during the Greig Middleton Ladies' Open race at Horseheath.

Right: Andrew Merriam receives the George Long Challenge Cup from Andrew Gooderham, left, after Royal Banker won the Restricted race at Horseheath.

pilot with a bright future.
 As for trainers, the Turner family enjoyed its usual solid campaign and the Sporborgs returned to winning ways after their barren 1999 season without ever threatening to touch the heights that had been achieved before being struck by the virus.
 Mike Bloom made an important contribution to Nibby's riding championship.

Ruth Hayter also provided her owners with plenty of silverware, a last-day double giving her principal patrons Anthony and Sue Howland-Jackson their 50th pointing success.

Pick of the area fixtures was the Cambridgeshire Harriers Hunt Club meeting at Cottenham where the highlight was Secret Bay's triumph in the Men's Open following the fall of Real Value.

Above: High Easter fence stewards get their instructions near one of the impressive obstacles.

Left: Easton Harriers secretary Janet Baxter, centre, with Ann Langley, left, and Jill McVay at High Easter.

The race of the season was in the Essex Hunt at High Easter on May 6, the final fixture of the year. Copper Thistle arrived at the Men's Open unbeaten in 14 starts only to find the combination of Dawn Alert and jockey William Wales marginally too good for him.

Taking on Copper Thistle fully a mile from home, Dawn Alert landed over the last more than a length in front.

Above: Parsons Way and Chris Gordon lead eventual winner Thats Dedication and David Robinson early on in the Tony Cooper Confined race at scenic Rodmell in Sussex.

Left: David Evatt receives the Challenge Cup from Julia Caffyn after Easters Eve won the Hunt race at Rodmell.

Copper Thistle showed the courage of a true champion to storm up the run-in but William is one of the strongest men around in a tight finish and Dawn Alert held on to land a famous victory by a head.

The weather gods were generous, with the odd exception, and there were decent-size fields and competitive racing right from the usual crowded curtain-raiser at Cottenham in mid-January through

Below: Following his breathtaking win on Thats Dedication Rodmell landowner David Robinson came back down to earth with a bump when Galaroi became a casualty in the Men's Open.

to the epic downfall of Copper Thistle's colours at High Easter.

The only meeting lost to the elements was at the notoriously ill-drained Northaw circuit and firm ground blighted no more than a couple of mid-season fixtures allowing those horses who need to hear their hooves rattle a brief moment of glory.

Although the 2000 season could be described as disappointing for Julian Pritchard after his three-year reign as champion jockey ended, the Ledbury-based rider still had much to be proud of.

Above: Clive Storey and Shay Gap part company during the Confined Maiden race at Corbrige in Northumberland.

Below: Alan Coe underlines his talent by partnering the bridleless Glencloy over the final six fences to finish third in the Open Maiden race division two at High Easter.

Above: Carlinare and Luke Morgan fall at the last during the Maiden race division one at Friars Haugh.

He rode 28 winners with West Midlands trainers Nicky Sheppard, Jelly Nolan and Jim Callow providing the majority of his successes.

Nicky has a good record over the past five years with horses that have been moderate performers with their previous trainers but she has been able to transform them into very successful point-to-pointers.

Dawn Invader benefitted from that talent this year with the nine-year-old son of Fine Blade winning at Dunthrop (twice) and Garnons.

Above: Shirley Vickery and Julian Pritchard lead the riders out of the delux changing rooms at Cheltenham for the Christie's Foxhunter Chase.

Below: Michael Miller, rider of Skip'N'Time, with his father Richard testing the Cheltenham going.

Above: Cheltenham riders (from left) Julian Pritchard, Ben Hitchcott, Adrian Wintle and Mark Bradburne.

Right:The Christie's Foxhunter runners head down the back straight at Cheltenham with Cavalero and Alex Charles-Jones (third left) getting a rear view of most of the field.

Above: The remaining Foxhunters head for the last fence with front runner Lakefield Rambler and Polly Gundry bravely hanging on to their lead. Mighty Moss (Fred Hutsby), right, Real Value (Ben Hitchcott), Trade Dispute (Grant Tuer), It's Himself (Andy Martin) and Knight of Passion (Pip Jones) are all ahead of the eventual winner Cavalero and Alex Charles-Jones in John Manners' blue colours.

Right: Audrey Manners leads in the Christie's Fox-hunter winner Cavalero and Alex Charles-Jones.

Above: Winning rider Alex Charles-Jones.

Right: Jockey Club spokes-man John Maxse, left, and Cheltenham Clerk of the Course Simon Claisse assess the opposition as they wait to race in the NFU Restricted race at Badbury Rings.

Below: Restricted race winner Dear Emily (Simon Claisse) races lady rider Mouse Barlow on the grey Another Junior during the first circuit at Badbury Rings.

*Co-Pilot wrote;
.... Following several near misses on the Ringwood Road, Troy, Co-Pilots new driver failed to see the Wimborne Minster turn off - an event which meant a compul-sory visit to the architecturally hideous seaside town of Bournemouth... Co-Pilot ventured down to the second last for the Restricted race, only to wit-ness the somersaulting fall of Another Junior and young lady rider, Mouse Barlow. The horse was quickly on his feet and head-ing back to the boxes but Mrs Barlow remained vertically chal-lenged until Co-Pilot- whose first aiding skills are legendary- con-cerned for the lady's well-being, approached with the intention of loosening the clothing. This course of action was nipped in the bud by a serious looking St John ambu-lance person no time had Mrs Barlow signalling to the crowd that she was uninjured.*

61

Left: Colonel Hogg of the King's Own Scottish Borderers presents the Gibson Cup to Phillipa Shirley-Bevan and Caroline Cox, centre, after Senso won the Maiden race division two at Friars Haugh.

He looked to have the beating of Lakefield Rambler in a hunter chase at Cheltenham before sadly breaking down during the race.

Upton Adventure was a major contributor to the Eastnor stable's fortunes with four victories while Capstown Bay, Black Oak and Ard Na Carrig also scored once apiece. Cowanstown Prince improved throughout the season finally opening his account at Paxford

Above: Kendor Pass, ridden by Nicki Wilson, lead the Ladies' Open field at Hutton Rudby in Yorkshire.

and could mature into a useful performer next year.

The Sheppards have purchased several new inmates at the summer sales and it will be surprising if they do not add to the yard's excellent record in 2001.

The colours of Patricia Duncan and her daughters Caroline Mackness and Vanessa Ramm have become familiar on West Midlands courses in recent campaigns.

Above: Rainbow Times and Clive Storey jump between dead-heaters Geordies Express (Andrew Richardson, left) and Excise Man (Jimmy Walton, far side) at Friars Haugh.

Left: Corbridge judge Nigel Murray, left, and Bob Neill declared the Men's Open a deadheat.

The bulk of these horses are stabled with Jelly Nolan at Winstone, near Cirencester, but they also had Irish hunter chase winner Sharimage and the enigmatic Idlewild with Nicky.

Soft ground curbed the flow of winners from the Nolan stable early in the season but their record improved as conditions firmed up. With Mounthenry Star, Jimmy Greenspoon and Arctic Grey returning after a year on the sidelines, the new season could see winners starting to flow with

Above: Pharmistice and Nicola Stirling, far side, jump with Sharp Thyne (Maxine Bremner) to take the Ladies' Open race at Friars Haugh.

Right: Friars Haugh rider Jamie Alexander with his brothers Nick and Michael after Fordstown won the point-to-point Club race.

greater regularity for the Cotswold set-up.

Fresh Prince was the best of the older horses during the latest campaign although Full Score and Haughton Lad also had their moments.

Happen To Make It, Catechist, Goawayoutofthat, Crafty Phantom and Mick Mackie made their debuts for the stable with only Catechist and Crafty Phantom, a half-brother to Copper Thistle, failing to appear in the winner's enclosure.

65

Above: Teeton Builds (Andrew Sansome) jumps ahead of Ruperts Choice (Simon Sporborg) and eventual winner on the far side, Hatcham Boy, ridden by Chris Ward-Thomas, during the Greene King Plc Men's Open race at Horseheath.

Tom Scudamore struck up a rewarding partnership with Glevum. The eight-year-old mare is trained by the rider's mother Marilyn at Naunton, Gloucestershire, and they were invincible during the early weeks of the season netting six consecutive races between the flags before being beaten by Slew Man.

Scudamore has been honing his talents with Martin Pipe during the summer and hopes to team up with Pipe's son David in the New Year.

Belinda Keighley and Dolly Maude - both wives of NH jockeys - chalked up their first point-to-point victories, Belinda partnering the Dolly-trained Newton Point to success at Barbury Castle.

Dick Baimbridge, who has been saddling winners from his Berkeley stable for the past 20 years, continued the flow.

Rip Van Winkle atoned for last

Above: Cool Yule and Wilson Renwick lead Ensign Ewart (Clive Storey) to win the Men's Open at Corbridge in Northumberland.

Right: Proud owner Rob Kyle and stable lass Amy Warden with Cool Yule after his Men's Open victory.

year's disappointments with four wins including the Lyon Trophy while Split Second bagged four races in the twilight of the season after a slow start.

Nether Gobions has been a wonderful servant to Baimbridge and there were a few moist eyes when the front-running 14-year-old, under Julian Pritchard, triumphed at Bredwardine three weeks after his owner Pearce Clutterbuck had passed away.

Well Ted looks a ready-made replacement for his veteran stablemate in Open events.

Co-Pilot wrote;

Resisting the temptation to stop for purchases at the sign near Flaxton advertising Christmas trees for sale only £6.00, Co-Pilot arrived shortly after noon at Whitwell-on-the-Hill - Troy having made up the time lost during an unnecessary incident on the M1 with a Spanish juggernaut.

....set off down the steep grassy slope to test the going. Striding out, once level ground was reached, Co-Pilot soon arrived at the legendary ditch estimated to be at least five feet deep. An off-cut of orange skirting-board lying on the grass would not do for these racing folk...

Shortly after Lord Grimthorpe had presented the cup to Brown and Duxbury, Co-Pilot was called upon to make a reflex save, as an elderly lady being gravitationally inconvenienced, wobbled backwards on the steep slope and looked in danger of cartwheeling down to the last fence.

The smile of relief and pleasure from the rescued damsel, and invitations to ....

further refreshment sent Co-Pilot scuttling to the relative safety of the bookmakers' lines.

Left: The Champagne tent does a roaring trade as a huge crowd basks in the Sussex sunshine at Rodmell.

Following two early-season defeats he scored emphatically at Andoversford and Paxford, being particularly impressive on the latter occasion.

Forest Fountain and Philtre provided Jim Callow with cause for celebration. Forest Fountain won at Larkhill before being an also-ran at Haydock and the experience gained at those venues helped him take a Stratford hunter

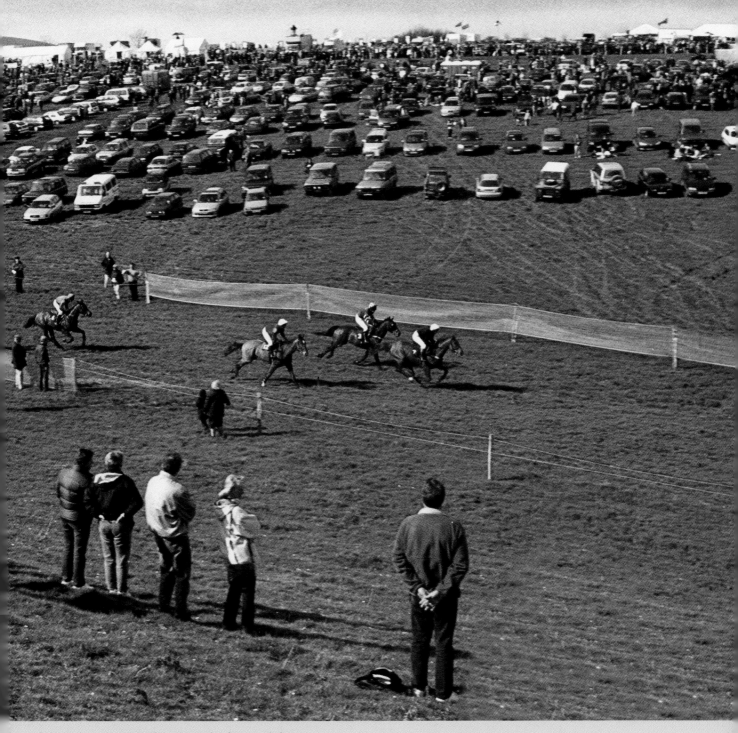

Above: A vast crowd enjoys the beautiful setting at Rodmell where the Restricted race field is headed by Nattico, ridden by Sarah Gladders.

chase later in the season.

On his 1999 efforts Philtre looked certain to bag a Maiden and this prediction proved correct when he triumphed at Whitwick and again at Chaddesley. The best could be yet to come from the Phardante six-year-old.

Point-to-point history was made in the South Wales area at the Brecon and Talybont fixture at Llanfrynach when a 14-race meeting beat the previous 13 races set at the same course in 1995. Full marks to the stewards in coping with six and a half hours of racing!

Above: Badbury Rings where a large crowd watches the Countryside Alliance Novice Riders' Club race.

Above: Kathy Dowling of Greig Middleton, left, presents the trophy to owner Peter Southcombe and his daughter Wendy after Olive Basket won the Ladies' Open race at Badbury Rings.

Left: High Noon at Badbury Rings and the Restricted race riders head for the showdown.

Evergreen Joe Price took the day's honours with a double on 20-1 outsider The Rural Dean and a division of the Maiden on his own horse It's A Handful. As The Rural Dean strode home in the first division of the Restricted, it was appropriate when The Archdeacon captured division three.

Llanfrynach has more than its share of controversy. Some years ago jockeys threatened to go on

Above: Restricted race contenders Bel Lane (David Jones), left, Howsyourluck) (Tim Vaughan) and Cresswell Quay (Grant Lewis) send the last fence birch flying on the first circuit at Llanfrynach.

Right: Grant Lewis, busy day at Llanfrynach.

strike as they were not granted car-passes and one year bookmakers downed tools, albeit for the first race only.

This time there were more mutterings when the hunt tried to charge grooms and owners travelling with their horse boxes.

Newport's Andrew Price and Evan Williams from Cowbridge landed trebles during the Curre at Howick.

71

Above: Dynamite Dan (Neil King), left, and Chris's Lad (Matthew Gingell), right, sandwich eventual winner Tom de Savoie, ridden by William Wales, during the HSBC Confined race at Horseheath.

The 29-year-old Price, riding his first three-timer, did the trick on Mags Super Toi, Chantingo Lad and Lillieplant while Williams' trio were Rave-On-Hadley, Cream Supreme and Twotensforafive.

Tiny Gemma Roberts, weighing just 6st 8oz, conjured up a surprise win on Robert Rowsell's Viardot in the Ladies' Open at the Monmouthshire at Llanvapley.

The 16-year-old, having only her second ride in public, came home by a distance on the 14-1 chance watched by a huge crowd.

Robert had to carry Gemma's saddle and weight cloth into the weighing-in tent as they were too heavy for the petite jockey to cope with.

Steve Blackwell, who has few equals in Wales, landed a

Above: Confined winners Parade Racer and Andrew Richardson, far side, follow front runners Charlieadams (James Muir) over the second last fence at Corbridge.

Maiden double with Rusty Buck and Bright Beacon while boy-wonder Christian Williams, now with Lambourn NH trainer Dai Williams (no relation), also had double delight on Kinnefad King and No Fiddling, a bargain buy for owner Steve Fisher who is mine host at the Pelican Inn at Ogmore.

John Milton's Karaburan, capably handled by 23-year-old student Fiona Wilson, outpaced his rivals in the Mixed Open at the Llangibby at Howick. Bought at Ascot two years previously for just 2,200 guineas, the six-year-old had four lengths to spare from Swinging Sixties at the line.

You Make Me Laugh put a smile on some faces when scoring in the Confined, appropriately on April Fools' Day.

Above: David Jones on Bel Lane is followed across the road by Evan Williams after the Restricted division four at the Brecon and Talybont Hunt meeting held at Llanfrynach.

Left: Record breaker - race 14 at Llanfrynach and the number board shows signs of distress.

Evan Williams, the eight-year-old's trainer, missed the ride through injury giving David Stephens the chance to land his 98th winner having returned to the saddle after hanging up his boots

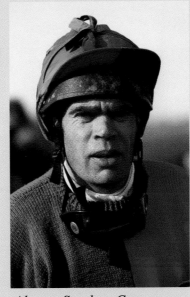

Above: Stephen Currey.

Above: Frank Windsor-Clive.

Above: Christian Williams.

Above: Hywell Evans.

some years ago.

The Glamorgan celebrated 30 years of pointing at St Hilary but then news broke that the hunt would be looking for a new venue in 2001.

One personality spotted enjoying a drink or two in the sponsors' tent there was film and television actor Leslie Phillips, who sponsored the Members' race along with his business partner Graham Nelson.

Above: Mr Kevernair and Mervin Woodward, far side, jump with eventual winner Millyhenry, ridden by Charlotte Tizzard, during the PPORA Novice Riders' race at Littlewindsor in Dorset.

Left: Former professional jump jockey Anthony Tory, now starter for the Wilton Hunt meeting at Badbury Rings. " 'Sir,' is about the only thing I haven't been called."

Christian Williams (African Warrior and Bannagh Beg) and Jamie Jukes (Flutterbud and Saffron Moss) both rode doubles at the fixture.

Kate Lovelace's long journey from South Dorset paid off when her Lucky Jim bagged a division of the Maiden at the Gelligaer at Bonvilston. Lucky Jim, who nearly lost a hoof after snaring his leg in wire, spent four months with

Above: Kinnefad King and Christian Williams, winners of the Confined race at Llanvapley, have a narrow lead over Tiger Lord (Andrew Price) at the last fence.

his leg in plaster and was the subject of a television pets' rescue programme.

Evan Williams, returning after a fall a month previously, recorded a four-timer (Marisol, Cream Supreme, Absent Citizen and Pull On).

Jason Cook - the 21-year-old winner of the novice riders' crown - recorded his first double at the rain-soaked Tredegar at Bassaleg on the pony-sized Anorak and Star Chaser and there was a significant milestone for the legendary Pip Jones who notched her 200th victory between the flags, albeit a hollow one, when Hal's Prince walked over in the Members.

A fine day's weather attracted a bumper crowd to the Banwen Miners' date at Pentreclwydau where the grand old man of Welsh hunt racing Jon Parry-Keen (Energy Man, Black Dan) and Evan Williams (Flockmaster, Saxon Queen) registered doubles.

In the rearranged Pentyrch at Bonvilston the Welsh Point-to-point Grand National - Wales' only four-miler - went to mud-lover Saffron Moss running over the trip for the second time in three days having finished eighth at Uttoxeter on the Wednesday. Owned by steward Ross Farr and ridden by Jamie Jukes, Saffron Moss caught Mostyn at the last.

Above; Griff and owner Isobel Smith lead Single Man (Susan Rodman) during the High Peak Hunt Members race at Flagg Moor where competitors face both Birch and natural stone walls, and left, Nick Fogg winning rider of Welsh Legion.

Lord Harry is being hailed as the best horse seen in the North West since Dover. But Midlands businessman Michael Parr, who owns the John Corbett Cup hero, is adamant that Night Irene, trained by Gary Hanmer at Nantwich, is the most exciting prospect and will turn out to be exceptional.

Racing in the area has seen the dawn of a new age with Gary

april

Above; Grimthorpe Gold Cup winner Prominent, ridden by David Easterby has the leaders in his sights during the 4 mile 1 furlong trip at Whitwell-on-the-Hill. Right;Michael Brown, Nick Duxbury and David Easterby after the trophy presentation by Lord Grimthorpe.

becoming the North West champion rider, ending Alistair Crow's seven-year stranglehold.

Alistair finished runner-up after the title race went to the wire with Gary settling the issue with a comfortable treble on Inglerise, Spumante and Garryspillane at the Wheatland at Wolverhampton.

The ladies' honours were retained by Carrie Ford, wife of Tarporley trainer Richard Ford.

Top: Traffic comes to a halt as the Confined race leaders head down the back straight at Flagg Moor in Derbyshire.

Above: John and Jackie Walsh, Honourable Secretaries of High Peak Hunt point-to-point held at Flagg Moor.

Right: Becoming soft, as Joanna Hughes leads Tessa Clark, left, and Jane Froggatt through a sea of mud for the Ladies' race at Flagg Moor.

Co-Pilot wrote:

Careering down the M5 to Somerset and the Paris of the West, diverting briefly to visit an old chum from the Marines, Co-Pilot was on course for Cothelstone.

All had gone well on the journey south until Troy, anxious to try out the new electronic system, had momentarily lost concentration at speed and left a caravan, being towed down the centre lane, swaying wildly across the motorway.

Squeezing up the narrow lanes near the course, past houses built of the local red stone, a colour Co-Pilot noted not dissimilar to the betel nut stains often seen in far-away places, Troy eased the motor into a space conveniently adjacent to the Secretary's accommodation.

Following a refresher with a small contingent from Dorset and leaving Troy to set lunch, Co-Pilot set off in the bright sunshine to walk the course. The finishing straight was in immaculate condition. The back section was fair but the area around the third last was fairly firm with some puddles on the slightly threadbare surface. The fences, though not the bulkiest seen lately, looked fairly unforgiving.

Racing was excellent and commenced with the seven runner Hunt race which David Luff won on Suba Lin. The blinkered Jollification won the Restricted ably piloted by Anthony Honeyball, but Co-Pilot's eye was caught by the dashing Charlotte Tizzard as she and Millyhenry blazed around the circuit, hardly seeing another horse during the Open race. Shortly after this event an announcement was made for all the photographers present to attend the Secretary's tent. The wretches assembled and stood around in the manner of magpies waiting for traffic to pass a piece of carrion, and Co-Pilot who had just emerged from the ladies' changing area, having mistaken it for the Tote, was astonished to hear their pitiful excuses when admonished by the course and fence official. In exceeding their non-existent authority in pursuit of their snaps, one swarthy fellow was apparently sighted driving his vehicle along the course during a race, a tall skinny character had been trampling through the early broad bean crop at will, and one elderly operator who looked as if he had fallen through a hedge professed to be collecting pictures for a book. These excuses were firmly dismissed, a flea was dispensed to the collective ears and without a word to each other the snappers dispersed.

The immoveable force and a hard place came together in the point-to-point Members' race in the form of Pipe versus Scudamore. The useful Bells Wood was passed three out and it was left to Tom Scudamore on his mother's Glevum and Les Jefford on David Pipe's Slew Man. In the end the more experienced Jefford prevailed and the runner-up, led in by acting stable lad Peter Scudamore, received commiserations from Martin Pipe on hand in the winner's enclosure for his son's success.

And so it came to pass that Co-Pilot and the others assembled in that muddy field witnessed the past, present and future kings of National Hunt racing gathered together at a West Country point-to-point. Something to tell the grandchildren.

It was same-again on the training front with Hadnall-based Sheila Crow finishing way ahead of her rivals with 26 winners between the flags and two under Rules with the peerless Lord Harry, who, besides his Stratford triumph, bagged the Bangor Final.

Once again a Sheila Crow-trained horse was champion horse for the area, the prize going to Weak Moment owned by the master of

Left; Glevum and Tom Scudamore after their defeat in the Point-to-Point Owners and Riders Association Club Members race at Cothelstone. Stable lad P Scudamore.

Right: "Mind if I borrow him for a few years?" Martin Pipe, who was in the winner's enclosure with his son David, advances on Tom Scudamore at the West Somerset Vale meeting at Cothelstone.

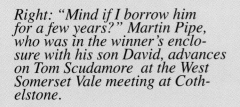

the North Shropshire Ian Hollows. Sue Norbury's Hatton Farm Babe was runner-up.

Champion novice horse was The Crooked Oak, owned and trained by Keith Thomas, secretary of the Vale of Lune Hunt, followed by Spumante, owned by Les Bush and trained at Malpas by Pete Morris. As for champion novice rider, the title was shared between Willie Hill and Joe Downes.

Left: John Boulter and Polly Gundry after Starpath won the Ladies' Open four-mile race at Flete Park, Devon.

Of the 15 meetings planned, all took place though the Tanatside went ahead after being re-scheduled which was a relief for the hunt as it had been lost for the previous three years. However, the fixture was marred by the death of their secretary Anne Jones, daughter of new area chairman Roger Everall.

The West Shropshire opened the season at Weston Park, which was a huge success in terms of atten-

Above: Newman's Conquest and Mark Sheares lead eventual winner Contradict (Sarah Gaisford), right, during the Exeter Inn Novice Riders' Intermediate race at a packed Flete Park.

Right: Sarah Gaisford after her victory.

dance, but because of dwindling numbers in the drag hunt's membership, this was its last fixture.

However, this early February date at the Shropshire course will not be lost because the Meynell and South Staffs are moving there from Sandon next season and the area will still have its quota of 15 fixtures because the North West Club meeting has been revived and will be at Tabley in May.

Action from Flete Park in Devon.

Above: Open Maiden race action at Paxford in Gloucestershire.

Left: Amanda Barnett on Pillmere Lad, right, battles with Tim Dennis on Damien's Pride during the Stanley Carpets' Restricted race at Flete Park.

The principal race in the area was the Scally Muire held at Wolverhampton's Dunstall Park racecourse. This Ladies' Open was won by Mouse Barlow on Ian Anderson's Killatty Player. But the most popular event was the Sandy Temple Flat invitation race, named in honour of the area chairman who died last year.

Alistair Crow took the riding honours on Harweld.

Above: Winner Furious Avenger, right, ridden by Lawrence Lay, holds a narrow advantage over My Nad Knows (James Baimbridge) during the Brewin Dolphin Restricted race in front of a huge Easter Monday crowd at Paxford.

Right: Everyone a winner - Cowanstown Prince connections line up with winning rider Julian Pritchard after the Open Maiden race at Paxford.

With the exception of the North Staffs at Sandon and the Holcombe at Whittington, every hunt reported bumper crowds.

North Staffs suffered due to the weather as not many people thought it would survive but a brave decision and plenty of hard work by clerk of the course Richard Froggatt and his team enabled racing to go ahead albeit in front of a sparse crowd.

Above: Decision time for punters at Whitwell-on-the-Hill in Yorkshire.

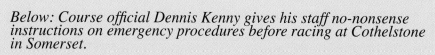

Below: Course official Dennis Kenny gives his staff no-nonsense instructions on emergency procedures before racing at Cothelstone in Somerset.

Above: End of the meeting at Whitwell-on-the-Hill and well trained youngsters set about tidying up.

The same reason affected the attendance at the Holcombe whose secretary Paul Knight attributed it to negative thoughts on the bush telegraph.

The South East invariably attracts entries from outside the area - especially East Anglia - and one runner travelled from as far afield as South Wales to compete in the Kent Grand National, the region's solitary four-miler which takes place during the West Street Tickham meeting at Detling.

The marathon journey for High Guardian was worthwhile too - but only after an objection. The judge announced a dead-heat between local horse Prime Course and High Guardian but after an objection by the latter's rider Julian Pritchard for "taking my ground at the last", the stewards awarded the race to the Welsh raider.

Left: The gentle-men's conveniences (before racing) at Whitwell-on-the-Hill.

Left: High Peak hospitality abounds in the gentlemen's changing room where nocturnal vision is a distinct advantage.

Below: Red carpet changing facilities for the gentlemen riders at Heythrop in Oxfordshire.

There has been bad publicity over the standard of horses within the area, something which owners strongly object to, and those stories were rebuffed in the best possible way with South East runners taking 12 hunter chases by mid-April.

Real Value, owned by Alan Cowing and Barry Cockrill and trained by Di Grissell, was the star of the season.

93

Left: Sue Young, all smiles after her Restricted win on Belittlir at Flete Park.

He took the scalp of the ill-fated Castle Mane at Newbury and was pipped by Cavalero in the Christies Foxhunters at the Cheltenham National Hunt Festival in March after a gallant performance in the very capable hands of his talented young rider Ben Hitchcott.

Di, herself a successful rider between the flags and under Rules, now has two daughters Coral and Hannah riding and both notched

A full house at Flete Park where If You Say So, ridden by James Young, leads the Greig Middleton Confined race field past the winning post on the first circuit.

wins during the season.

Another young pilot to make his mark was David Dunsden, a cousin to Findon NH trainer Josh Gifford for whom he rides. The partnership snapped up hunter chases with the likes of Loughnagrain and Finnow Thyne.

New courses are a rarity particularly in the South East but the Southdown and Eridge has moved from Heathfield.

Above: High Guardian and Julian Pritchard, left, Archies Oats (Jon Trice-Rolph) and Rusty Fellow (David Mansell), right, lead the chasing pack during the four-mile Men's Open race for the Lord Ashton of Hyde's Challenge Cup at Heythrop.

That meeting was relocated to Rodmell, near Lewes, which is farmed by one of the sport's great enthusiasts in David Robinson.

David's long-standing ambition was to have his own course - and not only did his dream come true but he rode a winner at its inaugural meeting!

Chris Gordon - champion rider last year - retained the award with the ladies' equivalent going to his

Above: Lord Ashton Cup winner Rusty Bridge with rider Richard Burton and lass Becky Crook.

Below: Professional jockeys Richard Johnson and Warren Marston amongst the mid-week crowd at Heythrop.

fiance Jenny Grant.

Veteran Jeffrey Peate, the popular trainer from Tunbridge Wells tbrought the curtain down on his career at the final meeting of the campaign.

As a rider he booted home 39 winners before going on to saddle 150 more as a trainer in an era spanning more than 50 years.

97

Bookmakers doing a roaring trade at Penshurst in Kent where a huge crowd turned out despite steady rain.

Michael Brown's Prominent, who went into many notebooks as one to follow after his 1999 campaign, lived up to expectations in the Yorkshire area.

The six-year-old, once an inmate of the Lynda Ramsden yard, landed four wins from five outings, his only defeat coming in a Mussel-burgh hunter chase. He began his season on the Witton Castle course early in February with a two-length

Intermediate victory in the capable hands of Kevin Prendergast from Primitive Man at the Old Raby Hunt Club.

The Badsworth fixture held at Wetherby saw a number of useful horses contest the three divisions of the Maiden, most impressive of which was the Marleys six-year-old Romantic Native who took the opening division but did not re-appear for the rest of the season.

Thirty-four years ago Brian Lee from Cardiff wrote a letter to the Horse and Hound complaining that point-to-points in his area were not being covered by the magazine. Hugh Condry, the then editor, gave him the job of covering them and since then he has been reporting on the sport for publications like the Racing Post, Horse and Hound and other national and regional newspapers. Here Brian describes a day in the life of a point-to-point correspondent:

It is 9.30 on a Saturday morning and the rain which has persisted for the last three days is still lashing down as I tuck into my two lightly boiled eggs.

Blast the telephone is ringing again. Ever since I jumped out of bed an hour and half ago the damned thing hasn't stopped. The voices on the other end all ask the same question: "Is it still on?" Bookmakers, friends and enthusiasts I don't even know all want to find out if the point-to-point will go ahead as planned.

And, being the South Wales area PRO, they expect me to know the answer. I give them the good news. Hardened point-to-point fans won't be put off by mere gales, snowstorms or earthquakes!

Breakfast finished, I look for my binoculars and dig out my wellington boots. Ten-thirty arrives and so does my friend Bob. We set off in his car and arrive about an hour before the first race. I always like to get to the racecourse early so that I can have a word with fellow race reporters, jockeys and owners.

As soon as the declarations go up on the numbers' board for the first race I note them on my race card along with the names of the jockeys, penalties and over-weights etc. After watching the horses in the parade ring I go across to the bookmakers to jot down the odds. Although there are no official starting prices at point-to-point, fans like to have some idea whether the winner was fancied or not when they read the reports.

With the horses going to post it is time to find a good vantage point from which to view the racing. The hardest part of the job - obtaining the order of all the finishers, horses that fell or were brought down, unseated and so forth - I now leave to others while I concentrate on interviewing the winning owners and jockeys.

The only thing I need after the interviews are the official winning distances and race time. If these are not announced over the public address system they can be obtained from the secretary's tent. The 35 minutes between each race goes very quickly. When I first started reporting on point-to-points five races a meeting were the usual thing. Now owing to the popularity of the sport, 10 or 12 races a meeting is not uncommon.

At last the meeting is over, but there is not time to hang around as I have to get home to write up my reports. The Racing Post's Hugh Condry and Horse and Hound's Carolyn Tanner will be phoning me sometime during the evening. It could be as early as 7.30pm or as late as midnight.

There have been some humorous moments over the years. All the riders in point-to-points are amateurs so I was tickled when one phoned me to complain about the not too complimentary comments I had made about his riding of a particular horse. After threatening me with a solicitor's letter he ended by saying: "After all it's my living you're writing about." Amateurs?

Contrary to popular opinion point-to-point correspondents do not spend all their time knocking back drinks in the sponsors' tent. I should be so lucky. On wet and windy days, when everyone else has taken refuge in their cars, they can be found, soggy race card in one hand and pencil in the other, trying to interview the rain-soaked winning owner or jockey in the unsaddling enclosure.

It has now come to a time that I am giving write-ups to the sons and daughters of the riders I was reporting on 25 years ago. Over the years, I have made many friends and met some interesting people between-the-flags. And to think it all really started that day 34 years ago when I wrote to the editor of the Horse and Hound.

Above: Winner Rip Van Winkle puts in a fine jump at the last fence for Alison Dare as The Bold Abbot and Sue West blunder their chance away in the Pel sponsored Ladies' Open race at Heythrop.

Left: Six times ladies' champion rider Alison Dare after her Heythrop triumph.

Ian Bray's Polar King, who won three of his four compeleted races in 2000, justified heavy market support in the second division thanks to a tenacious ride from David Easterby.

Probably the biggest gamble of the area's season was landed during the Sinnington fixture at Duncombe Park when Nigel Tutty's Murton Heights took the Land Rover Men's Open.

Left: Fiona Needham in the wars but still smiling after Pharlindo crashed out in the Confined race sponsored by Browns of York at Whitwell-on-the-Hill.

Above: With the sun low in the sky at Whitwell-on-the-Hill the last race runners head down to the start. The grey, The Happy Monarch, ridden by Fiona Needham, was last down - and first back in the Maiden division two.

Above: Ruth Clark.

Left: Chris Wilson.

Below: Richard Clark.

The ten-year-old, who has come back from two serious injuries, was backed down from 33-1 to 6-1 in this competitive race.

Murton Heights, ridden by his owner, was always travelling well and getting a good run up the inside coming to the final fence he stayed on strongly for a three-length win to justify that massive market support.

David Easterby's riding double

Above: Between races and time for enjoying the Yorkshire sunshine on the hillside at Whitwell.

was the highlight of the inaugural West of Yore point-to-point at Hornby Castle. The first leg came when the Ian Mason-trained Jackson's Hole completed a hat-trick in the Confined before Easterby struck again with Prominent.

This second race developed into a great but tragic battle with Sunrise Sensation taking a fatal fall when locked together with Prominent two out.

Above: Winners Highway Lad and Les Jefford, left, follow The Bold Abbot (Sue West) during the West Country Feeds Confined race at Kingstone St Mary in Somerset.

Right: Upton Adventure wins the PPORA Club race at Brampton Bryan in the hands of Scott Joynes.

Warwickshire raider Pharae made a succesful trip North to win the Ladies' Open during the Derwent at Charm Park in early March. Ridden by trainer Caroline Spearing the favourite made almost every yard of the running but he didn't have things all his own way as Marius ran a fine race in second.

Stephen Swiers brought up his century of winners between the flags when Mr Dick scored an easy

Right: Resting between races at Penshurst, from left, Tom Hills, Andrew Hickman, Paul Hall and Dominic Parker.

Below; Behind the scenes at Penshurst and the organisers deal with the paperwork.

Below: Policeman Paul Blagg gets his hands on the silverware at Penshurst after Kenny Davis won the Restricted race. John Absalom presents.

victory in the Men's Open at the Holderness.

Appreciating the fast ground at Dalton Park Jane Cooper's grey hardly had to get out of a canter to justify favouritism by 25 lengths.

The finish of the Confined was in complete contrast with Insideout reversing the form of their West of Yore meeting with Jackson's Hole when snatching the verdict in dramatic style.

107

Above: The effervescent Polly Curling and Kay Rees, left, with Intermediate race winner Sir Frosty, rider Richard Woollacott and stable lass Jo Buck, right.

Left: Cothelstone fences claim another victim.

Above: Suba Lin connections and rider David Luff receive trophies from Mrs Eva Davis of sponsors Greenslade Taylor Hunt, assisted by meeting secretary Margaret Brake at Cothelstone.

Pauline Robson notched the 100th winner of her career when taking the Ladies' Open during the Hurworth meeting at Hutton Rudby. Pauline, whose first winner came at Teesside Park in 1997 on Bantle Bowman, partnered the favourite La Riviera who won three races out of four starts this year.

David Easterby increased his lead at the top of the area jockeys'

Above: Bright Flash, ridden by Dennis Kenny, disputes the lead with Granstown Lake (James Young) on the first circuit during the Hunt race at Cothelstone.

championship with a double on Jackson's Hole (Confined), who was scoring for the fourth time this season in what proved to be his final outing of the year, and the front-running Pharstar, a horse he trains for this mother, in the fourth division of the Maiden.

The Jackson's Hole victory, however, was marred by the death of Insideout who fell when disputing the lead four from home.

Monkey Ago, trained and ridden by Jo Foster, picked up his third victory of the season by taking the Ladies' Open when the Bramham Moor Hunt held their meeting at Wetherby.

Above: Noble Hymn and Clive Mulhall, winners of the Mercedes Restricted race, separate Fiery Jack (Nigel Tuffy), left, and Never Wonder (James Tate), right, at Whitwell-on-the-Hill.

Right: Serena Brotherton with Lord Grimthorpe after the Grimthorpe Gold Cup at Whitwell-on-the-Hill.

In five starts this term the 13-year-old was never out of the first two - and this effort was probably his best of an excellent campaign by the evergreen son of Black Minstrel.

Feature of the Cleveland fixture at Stainton Vale was brother and sister Ruth and Richard Clark partnering both Open winners. In a race of veterans for the Men's Open - the youngest horse was 11

110

Above: Brampton Bryan winner High Bridge and Anthony Evans, right, jump with Rising Sap (Richard Burton) during the Restricted race division two.

- Richard triumphed on the Ian Brown-trained Private Jet, who although successful in a hunter chase, had never before won between the flags.

Ruth's victory came on John Mackley's Japodene.

Highly talented Key Debate made a hefty impact in his first season with five wins and a second from six outings - including two hunter chase victories. Before those hunter chase wins at Huntingdon and Hexham, the Tim Walford-trained eight-year-old signed off his pointing campaign when comfortably landing the Men's Open during the Staintondale fixture at Charm Park ridden by his regular accomplice Guy Brewer.

Above: Snow still visible on Titterstone Clee Hill at Bitterley as the Restricted runners begin their second circuit.

Right: Well Armed and Leslie Jefford power to victory in the Land Rover Men's Open at Flete Park.

Left: The Crazy Bishop and Ben Shaw lead Watchit Lad (Steve Blackwell) over the last to win the Men's Open race at Cursneh Hill, Herefordshire.

On the same card What A Fiddler - owned and ridden by Richard Tate - underlined his reputation as a bright prospect by completing a hat-trick in his debut season.

The seven-year-old won the 18-runner Restricted with plenty in hand and looks one to follow for 2001.

A double for Stephen Swiers was the highlight of the Zetland point-to-point.

*Right: Emma Lawrence and Clare Cul-
linane with Sam the rescue dog well
wrapped up for the Portman Hunt meeting
at Badbury Rings where sleet and gale
force winds kept all but the brave away.*

*Below: Hall & Woodhouse Confined race
leaders all jump well in the freezing condi-
tions at Badbury Rings. From left, Celtic
Token (Dom Birkmyre), Arbitan (Ollie
Elwood), Arfer Mole (Dan Dennis) and
Stoney River (Richard Young).*

Right: Grin and bear it. Arctic conditions prevail at Badbury Rings as Polly Gundry and owner Richard Williams receive the trophy from Mrs Mark Woodhouse after Abit More Business won the Confined race.

The David Easterby-trained Polar King set the ball rolling for Swiers at Witton Castle in the Confined before Not So Prim cruised home in the Restricted.

May saw the renaissance of Temple Garth who swept back to form with a vengence.

Above: Is this the exit? Mr Stackhouse calls it a day and Geoff Barfoot-Saunt waits for the crash.

Left: A battered Simon Cobden gets to his feet after Artful Aviator's crashing fall in the Eastbury Contracts Maiden race at Badbury Rings' last fence.

Below: Michael Miller survives an awkward moment as Silver Hill capsizes at the third last during the Clark & Partners Restricted Race at Badbury Rings.

Below: Peafield and Phillip York, left, jump with Glenpine (Charlie Weaver) to give owner and former Royal jockey Bill Smith victory in the Confined at Hackwood Park.

Above: Ladies' Open race field, sponsored by Exeter Investments Group, head down the back straight at Hackwood Park, Basingstoke, led by Emma Coveney on Strong Medicine with eventual winner Dawn Alert (Coral Grissell) green colours, left. Robin Gray commentates.

Above: Malvina MacGregor.

Above: Coral Grissell.

Above: Owner Clare Villar, right, and rider Chris Ward-Thomas receive the winner's trophy from Sarah Hill after Dry Highline won the Men's Open race at Hackwood Park, Basingstoke.

He achieved two wins and a close third in twilight of the season.

The 11-year-old sparked off his marvellous May run and left previous efforts for the year way behind by landing the Ladies' Open during the Bilsdale meeting at Easingwold in a thriller when owner Freyer Hartley got him up to pip Japodene on the line.

117

Above: A big turnout at Umberleigh fot the last meeting of the season.

Left: Emma James, left, with Sarah Jackson after Tee Tee Too won the SMB Ladies' Open race at Umberleigh.

Right: "Did somebody call?"

may/june

Above: Piggott impersonator Jamie Jukes on Itsstorm-ingnorma leads the Intermediate racers through a field of barley at Umberleigh in Devon.

The South West area saw a new course this year which must be the most southerly of all British Isles' courses, at Trebudannon, near St Columb Major in mid Cornwall.

After a lot of hard work by the owner and helpers, the opening day arrived but so did the rain'in torrents. Such a downpour created a slippery course and the meeting was abandoned after three races.

Above: Men's Open action at Peper Harow in Surrey where, far side, Boll Weevil (Stuart Robinson) leads Cut A Niche (Rory Lawther) and You Said It (David Crosse), left.

Right: The race commentary position of David Rhys-Jones at Peper Harow.

Co-Pilot wrote:
Following a brief and unintentional trip around the dismal dual carriageways of Guildford occasioned by supermarket lorries obscuring Troy's view of the road signs Co-Pilot arrived at the beautiful park that is Peper Harow.
Passing by the sizeable fishing pond and through the Saxon arch entering the course Co-Pilot was delighted to see the chestnuts, the copper beeches and the oaks dressed in their best spring clothes. With the sun already unexpectedly hot the motor was parked under one of the many cedar trees conveniently close to the secretary's tent.
The going was firmish in places but soft as expected near the area helpfully marked on the racecard map as bog.
The mercury still rising, the queue for ice creams estimated at 50 yards, and the beer tent impregnable, Co-Pilot was forced to take refuge from the fierce heat and stifling humidity in the champage tent, which was less crowded as only paper money was required.
In a packed Restricted race Hightec Touch crashed through the ditch in spectacular fashion. His rider Dan Dennis cut a lonely figure as he was left to wander back unassisted through the crowds clutching a wad to his cracked and bleeding nose, his swollen eye already partially closed.
The day's excellent racing was accompanied by a splendid commentary from the cherry picker by the royally connected David Rhys-Jones who, upon seeing lightning flashes all around announced his intention of immediate resignation should the approaching storm get any closer. The lightning subsided but Co-Pilot noted that Rhys-Jones thereafter only elevated the machine to half its normal height.

The celebrated Butler John didn't like the wet weather either and Westcountry Lad pipped him by a neck.

The course is a wonderful venue, provided by a great point-to-point

Above: Jojo and Colin Sherry lead as the Confined race field under the boughs of a huge oak tree gracing the course at Peper Harow.

Left: Peper Harow winner Emma Coveney.

enthusiast in John Welden. It is situated in beautiful countryside with fantastic viewing facilities and watched over by retired pointers, which look on from neighbouring fields with that air of "been there", "done that", "worn the bridle" attitude.

If spectators thought they would witness a moment of point-to-point history at Umberleigh on June 10 they were disappointed.

Above: Dont Tell The Wife and Gemma Hutchinson in full flight during the Members' race at Dingley.

Co-Pilot wrote:
After missing the turn at Rothwell when Troy was distracted by a giddy of lady cyclists on the A14, Co-Pilot found himself submerged in the red brick town of Kettering in the heart of Northamptonshire where until a few years ago employment opportunities in the local paper here normally contained numerous advertisements for Skivers. Sadly most of these jobs have now been lost, mainly to the factories of Eastern Europe.
With ample time available due to Troy's excessive use of the turbo charger on the M6, a comfort stop at Charles Wicksteed's famous park was decided upon. The park's home made ice cream, produced long before the American hippies had their big idea, tasted as wonderful as it had done when Co-Pilot wore short trousers. Though disappointingly, the paddling pool, a summer time treat whose glistening blue tiles and sparkling water had been so alluring nearly fifty years earlier now contained only sand and resembled a huge cat litter. Nostalgically challenged, Co-Pilot allowed himself to be led back to the motor by the yawning youth.
Arriving a short while later at the delightful but horizontally inconvenienced venue of Dingley just in time to secure the last remaining space on level ground, Co-Pilot left Troy to organise lunch and headed down the steep grassy slope to the racecourse.
The overnight rain had left the course fresh and in a couple of places softish, but the ground was generally in first class order and the dark fences fairly stiff. Feeling the effects of an interrupted night Co-Pilot decided to avail himself of a short cut along the vehicle track between the third and fifth fences. This course proved to be something of a minor disaster when nearly a foot of water lying hidden in the long grass ambushed the brogues and resulted in the rest of the walk being taken to the accompaniment of embarrassing squelching sounds.

The last meeting not only in the area but throughout the entire fixture list saw newly-crowned national champion Leslie Jefford start the day in Devon on 42 winners - one short of Julian

122

Above: Nuns Cone and Tim Lane (number 28) jump with Ebullient Equiname (Stuart Morris), Tiderunner (Simon Walker) and eventual winner Hostetler (Katie Norris) during the Confined race at Dingley in Northamptonshire.

Pritchard's all-time record. With a selection of rides on the Barnstaple track, the jubilant Jefford looked set to chalk up the best ever score but not even the advantage of being on home ground could help him achieve it after he gained one victory to stand on an equal footing with Pritchard. Jefford duly gained success number 43 thanks to the front-running Brave Noddy in the Open.

The envy had grown too much for me to handle. It was time for positive action, or in the words of that sports company advertising slogan: Just Do It.

I had always imagined what a thrill it must be to see a horse in my own colours win a race. Over the years I had watched the joy of so many people in National Hunt racing or between the flags around that winner's enclosure. Being part of a scene like that was my dream.

Now I had decided to do something positive to make the dream become reality. First step: find the horse, next put down hard cash to buy it - and then pray that you've bought shrewdly and splashed out on a donkey.

I had wanted to have my own point-to-pointer for more years than I care to remember. Somehow there always seemed a better use for my spare funds, like an exotic holiday, a new car, new carpets or, heaven forbid, another personal insurance policy.

But working on the premise that no-one on their death bed utters the words "I wish I'd spent more time at the office", I reckoned it was high time I fulfilled a long-standing ambition. After all, I wasn't getting any younger.

Fed up with working incessantly without having any real fun, I craved light relief and plenty of it. And I wasn't worried about how much I squandered, or rather "invested", in search of my equine goal.

I discussed it with my financial adviser. I would purchase these shares, that PEP and probably a bond. "But what about the rest of your money?" he inquired. "I'm going to buy a horse."

"Let me buy you the shovel,then," he said. "What will I need that for," I continued. "Because you might just as well dig a hole and throw your money into it," came his reply.

Buying a horse would give me no guarantees, would, I am sure, cost a lot more to train than I had bargained for and was not the sensible thing to do for a man hardly

An Owner's Life
by
David Briers

rolling in bundles of notes.

But no matter. My mind was made up.

Along I went to the yard run by the Alner family at Hazelbury Bryan in Dorset. Robert is a man steeped in point-to-point tradition as a courageous rider with 211 wins to his credit, a national championship to boot in 1992 and more recently as a trainer between the flags and under Rules.

He specialises in steeplechasing and is as straight as a dye. Just my kind of man.

"What sort of horse are you looking for?" he asked. "One that will give me some fun - and probably pick up the Cheltenham Gold Cup and Grand National along the way," I answered. Evidently that's what all owners want.

I was escorted round several animals, some of whom were available as a whole lot or in partherships or shares. But when one particular bay, fresh over from Ireland and barely backed, was led out of its box and stood as erect as if in the show ring, I knew I wanted that one.

Perhaps I should have vetted him or taken time to watch his paces or even see him jump a fence. But no. We talked money. Out came the cheque book and the unnamed five-year-old was mine.

That was only the beginning. Having ruled out an education in hurdling, we decided on the point-to-point route and he qualified with the Portman to run between the flags.

The following spring Woodlands Beau was set for his debut in a maiden at Larkhill. The first thrill came when he was led into the parade ring but that turned to a tingle down the spine when Tim Woolridge, wearing my green and white diamond silks, actually got into the plate.

I had done it. My own horse running in my

own colours. However, then came something I had not bargained for - fear.

Fear of my horse, who I had grown quite attached to since we were first introduced 10 months ago, getting hurt or worse. It was at that point I turned ashen and started wondering why I had spent all this money to put myself through this suffering.

The race started and two went down at the first fence. One fallen rider seemed to be in green - surely not disaster at the very first fence? Thankfully no, but we didn't get any further than the third - badly baulked and subsequently refused.

No damage done. Just a fraught introduction. And that timeless owner's adage "months of misery, minutes of elation" wafted through my mind.

Three more runs in maidens produced neither misery nor elation that season with respectable placed efforts.

But it was on a day early in the following season when Siberian winds visited Barbury Castle that I experienced the thrill of a lifetime. And it WAS worth the wait.

Woody and JD Moore, stable amateur at the Alner yard, had bonded promisingly on the home gallops. What's more their partnership flourished on the track as they swept into the lead turning for home.

The fear factor had again turned me ghostly white in the early stages of the race. But close home with pulses racing and heart pumping overtime, I thought this is the moment where the elation bit kicks in.

But no, Woody's sheer inexperience when in front saw him start wondering around an imaginary corner instead of running straight.

At that point enter Cavalero as if jet-propelled. He appeared from nowhere and strode past us but now that Woody had some company, he put his head down and began racing again.

Into the last fence the two protaganists went with JD making up the lost ground. Seconds later it was all over as Cavalero muffed it and ditched his rider leaving JD to stride home unopposed.

And oh yes, the adrenalin and the elation flowed. Torrents of it. It may only have been the novice riders' race but for all I cared, it might just as well have been a Gold Cup finish.

That triumphant feeling is marvellous and it is worth the wait and the frustrations along the way. Go get yourself a horse and try it some time.

Right: The joy of being an owner is demonstrated by Billie Thomson with her beloved Balisteros and rider Jill Wormall after one of his 13 wins this year.

Charlotte Tizzard and prolific winner Millyhenry in action at Cotley Farm in Somerset and, left, Charlotte in the winner's enclosure.

Above: Little Brockwell and Luke Morgan take off during their winning run in the Men's Open at Aspatria in Cumbria.

Just how effective Jefford was in South West territory was amply demonstrated at Buckfastleigh during February when he celebrated the first four-timer of his life, all of them being saddled by David Pipe. This meeting saw Jefford back with a vengeance after being sidelined by his Larkhill tumble with wins aboard Well Armed (Members), Iranos (Open), Versicium (Maiden division two)

Above: Riverside Run and Jimmy Walton lead Dennett Lough (Clive Storey) at Mosshouses to land the Men's Open race.

Right: Pharmi-stice and Nicola Stirling at full stretch win the Ladies' Open at Corebridge in Nor-thumberland.

and Horus (Restricted division one). Bratton Down in April gave Jefford two more winners on a day which brought the champion to-be more downs than ups. He triumphed on Ardbei (Intermediate) and Iranos (Confined) but fell twice and suffered an unexpected reverse in the Mixed Open when Horus surrendered his unbeaten boast on the taxing run-in.

Left: Baran Itsu with Paul Sheldrake in the saddle leads the Restricted field through the woods in the rain at Bassaleg.

Above: The umbrellas come up at Bassaleg but steady rain failed to dampen the spirits of the enthusiastic Welsh crowd.

Right: Halls Prince (Julian Pritchard), out for the second time in the afternoon, follows Rave-on-Hadley (Evan Williams) during the Confined race.

The drama on the final day of the South Midlands season surrounded Rory Lawther who clocked up a four-timer at Kingston Blount to depose Jimmy Tarry as the men's area riding champion.

Blacksmith Lawther began the day on a winning note with the odds-on Lucky Joe (Members).

Above: Smile Pleeze and Richard Burton in the unsaddling enclosure after winning the Men's Open at Eyton on Severn near Shrewsbury.

Below: Bredwardine winner Tim Stephenson.

He improved it with Castle Folly (by 15 lengths in the Open) and Dark Challenger (Restricted) but then had some nervous moments before hearing that he had kept the Maiden on Have A Break after stewards investigated interference between the five-year-old and runner-up Tonrin who had been separated by a neck at the line. Lawther might have matched Tarry's five-timer feat of 1999 had

he had the leg up on Castle Arrow but Julian Pritchard was in the plate as the seven-year-old landed the Confined.

Rusty Bridge is anything but rusty at the age of 13 as he proved by winning the four-mile Open from 15 rivals in April at Dunthrop which staged the Heythrop meeting, one of the few midweek fixtures on this year's calendar.

Above: Moondyne (Joe Price) heads the grey Persona Pride (Robert Hodges) during the Mills Whitcombe Maiden race division three at Bredwardine.

Below: Golden Valley officials Liz Thorneycroft (timekeeper), Will Holland (honorary secretary) and Chris Davies (announcer), right.

Above: Winning owner June Clutterbuck receives the Eddie Price Trophy from Colin Thomason after Nether Gobions won the Men's Open at Bredwardine.

This grand old character thrives on his racing - especially in the marathons - and he led virtually all the way before producing a game effort at the business end of the race to hold Rusty Fellow's challenge by five lengths.

Another teenager caused an upset at Mollington. The timeless racing adage is "back the outsider of three" but on this occasion it was the outsider of four after Kites

134

Above: Restricted race action at Bredwardine where Cead Mile Failte (Frank Windsor-Clive, 8) and Native Rambler (Clare Stafford) dispute the lead.

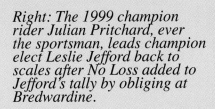

Right: The 1999 champion rider Julian Pritchard, ever the sportsman, leads champion elect Leslie Jefford back to scales after No Loss added to Jefford's tally by obliging at Bredwardine.

Hardwicke took the honours.

After a long enforced absence the 13-year-old Sunyboy gelding returned this year but had hardly set pulses racing with two remote finishes and a pulled-up from three early-season efforts.

The pattern looked like continuing at Mollington over the first half of the Men's Open Land Rover qualifier until roused by his rider and part-owner Peter Sheppard.

Above: Hals Prince provides leading lady rider Pip Jones with her 200th career win by scaring off the opposition in the Members' race at Bassaleg.

Above: Welsh winner Jason Cook.

Above: Muddied, Sue Matthews.

In the space of three fences Kites Hardwicke went past his two remaining rivals - favourite Freedom Fighter having exited at the 12th - and eased clear to score by 20 lengths from Deep Refrain.

The drinks were on publican Sheppard that night - this was his first success.

Four was also the strength of the field at Chaddesley Corbett during April for the Lady Dudley

Above: Jamie Jukes riding Itsthejonesboy leads the the Open Maiden field as the going turns softish at the end of a wet afternoon Bassaleg in Wales.

Below: Commentator Hon. Chris Lee in the wet at Bassaleg where most of the scenic course is visible from the steep hillside.

Above: Judge Williams conveyed back up the hillside to his accommodation at Bassaleg.

Cup - sadly an all-time low for this prestigious West Midlands event which was sponsored by The Racing Post.

As at Mollington, the race saw the downfall of the favourite with the odds-on 1999 hero Solba never being able to peg back Distinctive, ridden for the first time by Adrian Wintle. The Orchestra gelding made all for an impressive victory by 20 lengths.a

137

Above: Fred Hutsby takes a heavy fall as True Hustler slips on landing at the ditch during the Open Maiden race division one at Umberleigh.

Left: Reassuring sight at Dingley but no customers this time for the County Air Ambulance.

This was the second course win of the year for the former National Hunter handicap chaser who had been partnered by owner Debbie Jackson to land the Harkaway Club race from French Buck in March.

Horse and owner might have followed up a fortnight later only for Debbie to suffer a shoulder injury when unshipped by Distinctive while leading at the unlucky 13th at Brampton Bryan.

Above: Gravity gets the better of Clive Storey as he is unseated from Highland Monarch at Aspatria.

Right: Rider Dan Dennis retires to the safety of the changing tent at Peper Harow after getting tangled in the hooves of his mount Hightech Touch who fell at the ditch.

After his victory Adrian teamed up with Distinctive again to finish an honourable 10-lengths second to another ex-National Hunt performer Coulton over two miles five furlongs in a Cheltenham hunter chase during May.

On 1997 form it would have been impossible to suggest that three years later Strong Chairman would win a point-to-point at odds of 20-1.

Above: Tabitha Cave, two winners at Cotley Farm.

Below: Bookies do their best to accommodate the huge crowd at Cotley Farm.

Above: Cornering well, Les Jefford on the eventual winner Team Captain leads Green Anker, Harveysinahurry, Sun Lark, RU Bidding, and Caundle Encore during the Maiden race division one at Cotley Farm in Somerset.

But that was the price of Robert Waley-Cohen's gelding when he outgunned Philtre by half a length in the Confined.

Three years ago Strong Chairman had won all five of his races between the flags before pursuing a National Hunt career for trainer Paul Nicholls but the Strong Gale gelding never cut much ice in loftier company and was sold for 20,000 guineas at Doncaster Sales.

Above: The ill-fated Castle Mane and Ben Pollock take the last fence and the prestigious Intrum Justitia (Horse & Hound) Cup at Stratford.

Above: Proud owner Charles Dixey, centre,with the Castle Mane connections after the Intrum Justitia (Horse & Hound) Cup.

He needed time to rehabilitate in the point-to-point world with his new connections and five races came and went before the Chaddesley success which gave regular rider Sam Waley-Cohen the perfect 18th birthday present.

Patrick Millington deserves full marks for sheer persistence after first-season pointer Fortune Hunter finally shed his maiden tag at the 12th time of asking in a busy

Above: The Horse & Hound Ladies' Hunters' Chase at Stratford and eventual winner Vital Issue and Jo Foster lead Bullens Bay (Fiona Wilson) and Native Cove (Susan Sharrat), left, and Nova Nita (Jill Wormall), right, with a circuit to go.

Left: Lucy Horner, rider of African Warrior, winner of the Marsh UK/TBA Mares' Club final at Stratford.

Above: Jo Foster Horse & Hound winner.

Midlands' area campaign for the son of Lycius.

After being pulled up on his opening two runs the chestnut was close up when falling at the last fence in his third run at Brocklesby Park in February.

Following that near miss Fortune Hunter seemed an inappropriate name for the horse who had anything but good fortune - until mid-May at Dingley.

Above: Alastair Crow and Lord Harry lead Balisteros (Jill Wormall) over the last fence to win the Weatherbys Champion Novices' Hunters' Chase at Stratford.

Left: Nick Craven and Richard Russell, left, present the John Corbet Cup and momentoes to Mr and Mrs Mike Parr and Alastair Crow after Lord Harry's victory.

In the six-runner, five to seven-year-old Maiden Fortune Hunter strode eight lengths clear after the second last.

However, that margin was shrinking drastically on the run-in as the energetic Millington, driving the gelding for all he was worth, held on by a length from Balmoral Spring with Craftbrook Marchesa a further three-quarters of a length back in third.

Above: The Cheltenham Foxhunters Trophy arrives at Stratford on PPORA luncheon day. John Manners leads, Audrey Manners and Noffee Charles-Jones half a length behind.

Right: The Point-to-Point Owners and Riders Association AGM well attended at Stratford Racecourse.

Travel agent Millington was quick to recover and was soon celebrating again barely half-an-hour later when the diminutive Polly Live Wire chalked up a first victory in her ninth race of the year and the 13th of her career.

Having been third at Fakenham and then runner-up at Clifton-on-Dunsmore in her two previous outings the El Conquistador mare continued her place progression.

145

Mickey Elliot

Messrs Bryan, Jefford, Stuart and Mrs Egalton

Richard Hunnisett and Mrs Dick Woodhouse.

Terry Selby

PPORA Awards 2000

Alex Greenhow

Martin Quirk, Tracy Habgood and Charlotte Tizzard

146

David Brace and Steve Boxall

Messrs Ward and Barton

Josie Sheppard

Nick Craven (left) and James Mahon

Nick Craven and Basil Young

Patrick Young,Martin Quirk and Lin Loggin

Above: My Best Man, ridden by Lawney Hill, leads eventual winner Prince of Saints (Zoe Turner), right, during the Ladies' Open race at Kingston Blount.

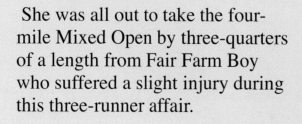

Above: Rory Lawther enjoys the winning feeling on the scales at Kingston Blount.

Above: Four wins in the afternoon for senior rider Rory Lawther at Kingston Blount.

She was all out to take the four-mile Mixed Open by three-quarters of a length from Fair Farm Boy who suffered a slight injury during this three-runner affair.

A season that contained many highs than lows saw the sport of point-to-point racing continue to grow in popularity throughout the country.

Confined race riders enjoy the sunshine at Kingston Blount with organiser Nick Quesnel, right.

149

Above: Up Your Street and Jason Cook lead Morgan's Rose (Martin Sweetland), left, and Holcombe Handsel (Anthony Honeyball) during Umberleigh's Open Maiden race division two.

Left: Robert Hodges, right, gives Hunt race winner Steve Lloyd tips on saddle carrying at Bredwardine.

It grew not only in terms of public and spectator interest but also with sponsors and the intrepid band of owners and riders, given a greater audience by television's Racing Channel.

Above: Georgetown and Leslie Jefford ahead of Ribbington (Olivia Green), right, and Outrageous Affair (David Mansell) at the top of the hill during the Captain Tim Forster Memorial Restricted race at Umberleigh.

Left: Lucinda Sweeting and Mr Custard enter the winner's enclosure at Dingley after the Ladies' Open race.

The omens were good right from the start when, even in the depths of January, warm sunshine and blue skies drew some 5,000 spectators to the first meeting of the new millennium at Tweseldown in north Hampshire. That set the pattern for a campaign made memorable for many reasons. For starters there were new national riding champions in Leslie Jefford and Polly Gundry.

Above: Scally May and Charlie Wadland lead the Intermediate field into the home straight at Chaddesley Corbett.

Above: Lorry park full at the popular venue of Chaddesley Corbett in Worcestershire.

Left: Judy Wilson and Mark Hewitt receive the trophies from Bob Hughes of sponsors Lex Land Rover after Barna Boy won the Men's Open at Chaddesley Corbett.

Then there was the emergence of rising stars Robert Biddlecombe and Tom Scudamore, two youngsters who have clearly inherited the ability of their National Hunt dads in the saddle. The continuing progress of Ben Hitchcott impressed many racegoers as did the training feats of David Pipe.

Right: Nothing Ventured and Al Beedles take the last in fine style to land the Members' race at Eyton on Severn.

Heavenly: Walking the course before racing at Umberleigh on the last day of the season.

Above: Nordic Spree and Rilly Goschen head the ladies' race on the first circuit at Peper Harow.

Left: Richard Young steers Here Comes Henry over the last to win the mixed Open race at Cotley Farm.

The exuberance of Balisteros and his 13 victories, the Cheltenham Festival brilliance of Cavalero and the Stratford triumph of Castle Mane only for the pointing world to be stunned by the death of Caroline Bailey's celebrity shortly afterwards.

The variation in equine and riding prowess is matched only by the difference in the courses and scenery throughout the country.

Top: Last day of the season and new men's champion Leslie Jefford gets the champagne treatment from fellow rider Colin Heard.

Above: New ladies' champion Polly Gundry.

Right: The end of another busy season for Patrick Millington - 83 rides and three winners.

Compare East Anglia with its flat courses, marvellous turf at High Easter and smattering of Newmarket types in attendance with, say, the basic facilities at some of the Welsh meetings.

But in whatever area, the enthusiasm and love for racing between the flags is as strong as ever - and not even a government committed to banning hunting can stifle those qualities.

Above: Balisteros and owner Billie Thomson safely back home at Lambden with the silverware. Photograph by John Grossick.

contacts

Point-to-Point Owners and Riders Association:
Secretary Jeanette Dawson 01227 713080

Point-to-Point Dept. Jockey Club 0207 343 3223

PPORA representatives
Devon & Cornwall: Keith Cumings 01769 550528
East Anglia: Pat Rowe 01799 550283
Midlands: John Docker 01203 332036
North West: Tim Garton 01625 584543
Northern: Gus Minto 01573 223162
Sandhurst: Simon Claisse 01367 850598
South East: Anthony Alcock 01233 812613
South Midlands: Chris Loggin 01869 810594
South Wales: Julie Tampin 01222 830278
Welsh Borders: Graham Saveker: 01432 343655
Wessex: Jeremy Barber 01460 74943
　　　　　Leonard Vickery 01963 440043
West Midlands: William Bush 01225 891683
West Wales: Cynthia Higgon 01437 731239
Yorkshire: Tom Bannister 01729 830206

Jockeys representatives
Midlands: John Sharpe 01832 731774
Southern: Grant Cann 01884 32284
Northern: Simon Walker 01132 892341

Point-to-Point Area Secretaries
Devon & Cornwall: Peter Wakeham 01364 643252
East Anglia: William Barber 01485 570983
Midlands: Mrs Karen Pickering 01469 588192
Northern: Anthony Hogarth 01896 860242
North Western: 01948 664977
Sandhurst: Philip Scouller 01491 574776
South East: John Hickman 01233 502222
South Midlands: Lucy Brack 01367 850598
South Wales: Colin Cross 02920 866453
Welsh Borders: Frank Morgan 01568 611166
Wessex: Franey Matthews 01747 840412
West Midlands: Robert Killen 01454 261764
West Wales Mrs Cynthia Higgon 01437 731239
Yorkshire: Mrs Sarah Stebbing 01677 424424

Talking Point:
news 09068 44 60 61
results 09068 44 60 60
fax entries/results 09068 44 99 88

Point-to-Point Sponsorship Committee:
chairman Nick Price 01327 860297

Nene Milling 01933 663965

Point-to-Point Web sites:
www.paleface-point2point.co.uk
www.thetalkingpoint.co.uk
www.jumpingforfun.co.uk
www.equestriancornwall.co.uk

paleface-point2point.co.uk

john beasley

Sincere thanks to the many contributors without whom this work could not have been produced. They include Tony Alcock, David Briers, James Crispe, Peter Elliott, Arthur Shone, Peter Mansell, Brian Lee, Fred Sampson and Richard Watts.
Special thanks to Jeanette Dawson of the PPORA and to Terry Selby of Chase Publications for their help and encouragement.